Ab

Ottawa-born, Vancouver resident, and member of TADS poets' group, Cath Morris's poetry has been published in *TADS*, *Urban Pie,* and *The Capilano Review*, and online poetry journals, *Ottawater.com (3rd, 8th, 10th, and 11th Issues), Poethia.com, and Bywords.ca.* Cath worked as a journalist for *The Georgia Straight* and *VAM Magazine*. Her first two chapbooks, *Venus & Apollo*, (2009), and *Fish, Ophelia, and Other Broken Dolls* (2018) were published by Pookah Press. Her work also appears in the west-coast poetry anthology, *Make it True: Poetry from Cascadia*, 2015, (Leaf Press, Nanaimo, B.C.), *Corporate Watch UK's 10th*

Anniversary Anthology (2007) in Oxford, UK, and the birthday tribute book to Canadian poet-laureate, George Bowering, *71(+) for GB* (2005). After moving out west after university, Cath worked in Vancouver as a journalist, a university writing tutor, and a television researcher/writer and script editor. She has also traveled the world with her beloved partner, recently deceased writer and mountain climber, Max Cutcliffe.

Dear Ivka, Faith,
Kylie, & Jules,

THE LOOMING

Lovely to meet you
I'd love your
feedback —
Cheers.
Cath
cathmo23@shaw.ca
Cath C Thoms

Cath (c) 604-817-5668
(h) 604-738-1169

Marnie ~~(604)~~ 775-877-9131
~~(604)~~

CATH MORRIS
___

THE LOOMING

Vanguard Press

VANGUARD PAPERBACK

© Copyright 2022
Cath Morris

The right of Cath Morris to be identified as author of
this work has been asserted by her in accordance with the
Copyright, Designs and Patents Act 1988.

All Rights Reserved

No reproduction, copy or transmission of this publication
may be made without written permission.
No paragraph of this publication may be reproduced,
copied or transmitted save with the written permission of the
publisher, or in accordance with the provisions
of the Copyright Act 1956 (as amended).

Any person who commits any unauthorised act in relation to
this publication may be liable to criminal
prosecution and civil claims for damages.

A CIP catalogue record for this title is
available from the British Library.

ISBN 978 1 80016 305 8

*Vanguard Press is an imprint of
Pegasus Elliot MacKenzie Publishers Ltd.*
www.pegasuspublishers.com

First Published in 2022

**Vanguard Press
Sheraton House Castle Park
Cambridge England**

Printed & Bound in Great Britain

Dedication

I would like to dedicate this book to my beloved partner, Maxwell Cutcliffe, who has taken me on a wondrous adventure around the world; to my best friend, Imelda Byrne, who has stood by me and helped in so many ways, for many years; and to my fellow poet and long-time friend, George Stanley, for all his brilliant and kind literary help over the years.

I would also like to dedicate this book to my beloved younger brother, Alan, who has been a dear friend for most of my life.

I would further like to dedicate this book to my dear older sister, Merideth, with whom I became closer later in life, and who sadly passed into the next realm in 2020.

And, finally, I would like to thank my brother, Alex, and his wife, Victoria, and their sweet family, for being there when I needed them in the last few months.

Acknowledgements

I would like to acknowledge the kind help of my beloved partner, Max Cutcliffe, and his loving family in Tasmania.

Contents

The Fog of Greed 15
Shards 18
The Academy 21
Alien Love 23
Ogres of Oligopoly 25
The Mystery 28
New World Order 30
Round 2 32
Solitary Tourist 34
Money is Murder part 1 36
Money is Murder part 2 Feb 2019 38
New Revolution 41
Non-Halloween Ghosts 42
Old Poem about Nature 44
Colonization Redux 45
Silhouette Maze in Play 48
Label and Destroy 50
Bella Luna 52
About Time 54
The Will 58
Chariot - for Maxie 61
We Gods 63
PART TWO 64
After the Fall 66

The Drowning Sea	71
Star Moths	73
Monopoly	75
Cleopatra in The Big Shop of Horrors	78
Motorless Replicant	80
Red Donkeys	83
Long Moons	85
Wolf Courses	87
When We Were Fish	92
Cobalt Blue – for Jack Williams	94
The Olive: An Ode	97
Four West Coat Haikus	99
Experiments with Sonnets	101
An Artist's Dream	102
The Ride	104
The Mountain Climber Who Fell Down in my Bathroom	106
A Pecunious Woman is a Harloty thing	108
The River	110
Adamantine	114
Wakener (to the great Haida artist, Bill Reid)	116
A Clump of Monks	120
Fulfillment	123
Symphony of Nothing about Sartre	125
Wounded	129
The Foggy Ant People Who Forgot	132
Gorby's Revolution	135
Hey Nonny Arabesque	137

O Please Don't	139
The Great Wall: *Fin de Siecle*	141
A Faint Roar	143
The Hall of the Drunken Fairies	146
Stardust Memories	148
Oh Cat	149
Argillite I	151
Faunic Triptych	153
London: Impressions	157

The Fog of Greed

these strange and salutary days,
when the media plays on the world's fears like a zither,
the fog has been thick with haze
as if to add to the gloom
a sense of eerie portent—
of muddled times
confusion in the highest minds

Shakespearean,
the fog warns of witches and foul deeds
performed in the darkling mist
manifesting our collective interior state

bubble bubble, toil and trouble,
now begins to burst the bubble

fog horns hum warnings
like huge unhappy waterbeasts
moaning for light and clarity

and even the darkest hearts
cannot help but think
of the inevitability of charity;

Eliot-esque, it comes
not on little cats' feet

but like Draconian dry ice
evoking the vampirism
of elitist capital
sucking the life blood from the common folk;

still the fog rolls in
like the guilty breath of giants,
steam from burning flesh
a shroud of smoke and mirrors
in which we all could choke

in these strange and salutary days
when no man or woman,
aristocrat or peasant,
can feel entirely safe
from complete system collapse
or climate change,

the Dickensian fog
hides the soot of poverty
the homeless problem – out of sight
the selfishness of shoppers
in a sleepwalking trance
through endless night;

beams from the streetlamps
shine hazy shafts
like searchlights through mist

reminding us that we, too,
are lost in the fog of avarice
befuddled, not yet kind

it represents our ignorance,
the cloud that girts our minds;
the murkiness, miasma,
confusion, stupor, daze,

in this bewildered smog,
how will we find our way?

January 25, 2009

Shards

we are the broken shards under the world;
forgotten palimpsests who breathe a secret message
only the initiated can decipher:

scholars, seekers, perceptive knights, who
when polished by the right hands, reflect light;

unrecognized, we've wandered endless night
for ancient centuries, unknown, unsung;
still, we wait, by candlelight,
by lonely docks, in corner bars,
beside old clocks, beneath the stars,
or *tremulous Celtic idols...*

cobbled streets still hide us; under lamps,
we meet in the clandestine damp; in dark rooms,
cybercellars, talk of slaughter,
the Message from Water,
with an anti-Darwinian slant;
watch the moon;

ubiquitous but few, ours is an obsession with the new,
the jagged mental glue that joins thoughts;

unfooled by the trick of time, we climb
the heart's ladders, search the Eddas for clues,

explore labyrinthine histories,
we're not much different than you;

no flesh-and-blood children fill our arms
no hearth or breakfast times;
we work alone,
like troglodytes,
forced to search for truth in the half-light,
eat cuttlefish and aubergine,
dig deep for our respite;

we saw it all too clearly,
the wrong directions, missing links,
dangers hidden in holy tomes,
needs that compelled mistaken coalitions
tendencies to form alliances against the strange;

the sticky damage that takes so long to repair,
wrongful notions that made the world unfair,
the longing that inspired empty deeds,
the paving of the village square…

saw, for instance, how despair
can do strange things to those in whom it broods,
making monsters of the hopeless,
children forged in schools of holy vengeance
perpetual cycle set in motion again,
breeding tomorrow's Machiavellians —

who take the twisted burden up
and roll it into a hard ball of hate
that, when loosed upon the world
leaves a desert of jagged shards
sticking out of the sand,
shining edges reaching for light
in the dark surrounding dust.

The Academy

bourgeois reductionists
creep through the halls of the academy
like guilty things
in love with the productions of legalized crime
skulking behind
the heavy wooden doors of opportunity
that knock knock knock
against young wooden minds

using the passive form
like a stealth weapon
to train, confound, define,
perpetuate the myth of objectivity

these anti-intellectuals
are eerily effectual at
slipping through the reins of responsibility
and, instead of teaching kids to think,
making little robo-capitalists
out of young-yuppy-yahoos
on bookish production lines;

in the guise of education
they teach them to ache for acreage
encourage measurement, analysis,
charts, means, paralysis,

instant gratification,
fear of the poor,
good times.

August 2007

Alien Love

the loneliness of greed
strikes hard
on the caring
and alert ones
crushes the hope of even
the oldest idealists

who remember,
try to revive,
the camaraderie of kindness
and the old goddesses' views
of all of us
floating in the same sea

the loneliness of greed
confounds
and saddens
the purer hearts
even the young

who have been taught to believe
that money is the only dream;
top scheme; the only benchmark
of human worth

it almost makes one want to

revive religion
but, sadly, somehow
those outmoded tracts
have become about something other than human love

LOVE
Human?
Alien?
LOVE

June 2016

Ogres of Oligopoly

there are too many ships in the sea
too many things one thinks that one needs
and it's making us crazy
to the bottom of the sea

why is a garment with a name on it
worth twelve times more than
a classic old sweater?

why can't I find my favourite foods
in the supermarket any more?
what's happened to the stuff that is better?

it's gone; where? I don't know
perhaps over the pond,
perhaps hidden in the melted snow

it's the ogres of the oligopoly
and the new capitalists' love of monopoly
(no timer on the game of greed
no attention paid to *actual need*)
who're laying us on the rising fire,
who're taking our lives based on misplaced desire

if (money) be the food of love, play on
give me excess of it,

*that surfeiting, the appetite may sicken,
and so die**

part 2

the orange red yellow gold
late autumn day

fills my soul with quiet hope
despite the terrifying times
of plastic nightmares
and unchecked selfish grope

in a culture gone off course
a capitalist colonial disaster
fashion and selfie-good-looks the main screed
the highest goals of the new generation
want more important than *need*

not even aware they are ravaging savages
oblivious young supporters of
the ogres of oligopolic greed
oil, coal, cars and carbon
groped from the earth
and rampant poison chemicals
foisted upon all our basic seeds

the rising *oil-igopoly*

raping and destroying all that we need

I feel sorry for the crow screeching in the thinning tree by the high e-coli drowning sea

wondering how this got to be

November 23-25, 2019

* Orsino, Act 1, Sc. 1, in Twelfth Night by Williams Shakespeare.

The Mystery

Why are we here?

to witness the soft-eyed stare of the squirrel
or the grumpy fish?
or the curious little bird
all reflections of some part of ourselves

to fear and control that sense of relation
a deep connection to alien species

or to fear that which is part of us
instead of that we find ourselves drawn to
for the wrong reasons

or is it the faces in the tiles (or carpet)
that look like those we knew
in one lifetime or the next
or those ex-lovers we've lost touch with
– and have never seen since –

or is it to learn how
to bring love into politics and power

my dear part-Sioux husband, Jack,
once put me at ease when I was in a state
for some reason – or was fearing death –

when he quietly (and somberly) said,

"You just have to learn to *enjoy the mystery*"

– the wisest words I've ever heard

'in times of trouble', that axiom,
and remembering my *connectedness to all living things*,

help calm me down

May 31, 2018

New World Order

I've noticed lately how swiftly things are changing
the First and Third Worlds merging
so it's all becoming more *streetish*,
busier, more stuff, less quality
dirtier, messier, more exotic,
more *carnivale*,
less village square
abstract, quixotic
heated up,
not so cool
less elegant,
less fair

this would be bearable if it meant
more sharing, caring
melding of hearts
and minds
but I fear the opposite is true and
most will get left behind

until we all melt
together
on the sidewalk,

like butter
(or sizzling bacon rinds)

August 2012

Round 2

round creatures in a square world
we are kept apart by lines
blinds, walls, doors
squares, rectangles, by design,
not meant for the geometry that keeps us in,
holds us prisoners in the
productions of our minds

soft creatures in a hard world
light shines through us
leaving us vulnerable
to the *thousand shocks*
sharp edges
rough surfaces
flesh is air to

hard creatures in a soft culture soup
of weak wills, feint hearts
lazy habits
lusty thoughts
fearful of love's wounds, its loss,
we become hard
square,
sharp,

blind,

cold creatures in a warm world

unkind

August 2007

Solitary Tourist

Slowly, carefully, I step into the picture frame and die...

I've travelled the four corners of the earth,
seen her towns and cities, by night, by day,
her trees and unusual valleys;
I've stayed awake until 9:15, 9:20, and 9:32
I've slept on beds whose lengths defy their heights
and hard definition
had a thousand million dreams in strange cities
no one will ever know or remember,
stood on strange street-corners where no-one
recognizes me—

the soul is a solitary being
except for its connections
which are unseen, unsensed by most,
mysterious, invisible, and oft in disarray

when does conscious experience become memory?
travelling, the two overlap,
like fading postcards on a hotel room bedside table,
and soon one begins to feel it is all only memory,
which George calls the inaccessible part of the mind;
(I think he means we can't search it,
it either bubbles up or it doesn't)

but, like the harbours, it begins to blur together,
life becomes a fast train
and memory its views
through fog-covered windows
on a journey of lonely discovery
others only barely glimpse;
and we are all just tourists
forever riding
until our stop

October 13, 2010

Money is Murder part 1

"Every gun that is made, every warship launched, every rocket fired signifies, in the final sense, a theft from those who hunger and are not fed, those who are cold and are not clothed." – Dwight D. Eisenhower

the crunching number culture is
crushing people
and money is killing Mother Earth
money is murder
life is magic
money is murder
greed makes it tragic
makes men want to hurt her

our mother, Ms. Earth, and all her compatriots
children, sisters, princesses, who, somehow,
from childhood, feel,
know
it is their duty to look after Her –
their mother, their lifeline,
their queen, their home,
their Natural Throne
every little bug a cousin,
every homeless wraith a son,

every rapist an alien – from another sun
or misguided book that put men first
at everyone's peril.

Money is Murder part 2 Feb 2019

raised to believe it was the benefit of honest hard work,
money is not a happy result
money is murder

money falls in murder's pocket
where it plots a new demise
at the great expense of management
it hollows out your eyes

money claims self-righteousness
as though all those who have it
are as good as gold
models of society
not greedy selfish trolls

they worked hard for the money
or they cheated, stole, and lied
some of the best thieves are educated
Harvard? Yale, anyone?
Wall Street?
drones in the skies?
learning how to plan for others' demises

in some ways, it's not their fault,
we live in a culture of greed

in which thieves are revered, like ministers,
the greedy promoted and feared

and numbers men win
and art is defiled
and bosses chew up
everything in the wild

deck the halls with troughs of money
fa la la la la
la la la la
'tis the season to be funny

money is mayhem
can break lives and hearts
tear loves apart
with its ruthless power charts

perhaps I do exaggerate
there are many honest folks
but the white-collar thieves and laundry men
damage the applecart spokes

it occurs we should perhaps return to
a system that worked quite well
the old commodity-barter one
where you're under no one's spell

but your own two eyes and little brain
show you exactly what's for sale
exactly what you're bargaining for
fair trade – not on the Wall Street floor

where shysters rule
the money domes
and, while destroying yours,
expand their own homes

Afterthought:

I'm hopeless, I'm hopeless
I cannot focus
and suddenly everything rhymes
It comes from reading Leonard's last book
and loving his non-nursery rhymes

and feeling the prick of his poetic hook
and that it's truly the end of best times

Fall 2019

New Revolution

The house of cards is falling – it's a new world!
Instead of bombarding us, they have to curry our
favour;
dark secrets are being revealed
the social network is transforming how we do business
and engage with each other
our Great Aussie Geek is keeping the hawks honest
exposing,
old covert acts of mercenary warlords
creating
the first real free press in more than a century,
a new transparency,
and the young are waking up,
and rising up
against the tyranny
because they can see everything
the corporate spiders have not yet strangled the web
but angels of truth prevail*
it is a new world
for all at once

Hobart, Tasmania/ March 2011
*(sadly, this turned out not to be true)

Non-Halloween Ghosts

so many ghosts
like wisps of smoke in the cold night air

and Halloween is coming
but these are not those kinds of ghosts
these are the real ones
the very quiet kind
who seem to call on you
in faint whispers
barely audible

murmuring like the TV next door
through the wall
but you can't make out a word

muffled by the other great wall
the Big Transition Wall

the dark
cold
slip-through-dimension wall

there you are again
human shadow on the blind

or down in the street

shuffling through the leaves
like lost children

stifled souls
of people I once knew and loved
and held
and kissed
flesh beings
with light in your eyes

and now
I barely have time to think of you

when I do,
I wonder what happened to you

October, 2009

Old Poem about Nature

oh my god
the rainstorm whispers and mutters
blowing its cool breath on my face
while the secret ceremony
screams and coughs
inside my temple walls
Nature takes hold,
cradling, refreshing,
and full of marvels
to quench my lonely hours

Nature, my sweet guardian,
I will always be yours
I have always been yours
not even death will alter that

1995/2016

Colonization Redux

what is this frightening feeling
this unease –
the Old Colonizers being colonized
so used to being the ones in charge
troubling
disquieting
culturally unsettling

this slow erosion of power through population alone
is a new world order
regime change
all the old traditions gradually being eroded,
with new ones in their place
brought over by the new lot
who've just fallen in love with Capital
the God of Money
ruling the globe

though not religious, I wonder
what happened to Christian kindness
help thy neighbor
not embezzle her out of all s/he has;

I worry about
non-citizens buying property and leaving it empty
because it's worth more that way

about the New World Order
in which only the fount of money rules,
the wealthiest pay no taxes,
and little-to-nothing trickles down

but wait! it suddenly strikes that
this may be a *Karmic* development
to teach the Old Guard
how it *feels*
to be *reacculturated*
(told what really matters)
after having forced their own worldview on the
original population here
and practically enslaved
the new dominant ones

whose hard work soon turned things in their favour
leading to the New Order
in which the Old Colonizers now find themselves
wondering how the greed culture
they encouraged
came back to bite them

left them disoriented,
groping for traditional foods and clothing that fits,
in empty stores on the high street;
sitting on overcrowded busses,
or in white, characterless cafés

that sell nothing but donuts
not as an act of revenge,
but just because that's what the ruling younger ant
mob wants
at present…

August 2017

Silhouette Maze in Play

there we were all of us lined up like a silhouette – a
human pattern on the bathroom mat, a painting, my
theme, my life, a silhouette: all heads and torsos
and behind
colours
a sunset
humanity knitted in a line
in black
in front
of
purples and pinks and yellow turquoise blues – a
sixties silhouette poster of hope and yours just one of
the faces on the horizon line like an ocean, each wave
tip a separate consciousness but down below all One
Big Sea (of humanity) – connected by light and love –
Jung's Universal-Unconscious; somewhere in other
worlds or universes still lined up along the hand-in-
hand, as it were, horizon which forever fades as we
forge on… we need a boat… in this vision I've been
seeing for years in my painter's eye, this sea… see
this… vain human…ity profane van…ity; forgive them
for allowing the green plant to let them see the sunset
properly, feel the insan-ity –

crop-souls in the misty drove, reckoning before their
time, reading Siddhartha and *Damien,* Steppen with

the Wolf, playing *The Glass Bead Game*, listening to *I Like to Dream* in a purple maze, Watts and Miller and Lao Tsu – people who knew, feeding you, reading Seth, Jane, Paramahansa Yogananda, meshing the comprehensive astral planes with the multiverse they feel now, lately – I mean, sense; can prove with math and everything – this new theory of everything, you, me and the baobab tree, tiny strings in the divine violin orchestra,
learning humility like Shakespeare and the brutal Pinter, the prescient Ibsen, sly Chekov, meeting gentle Tennessee (W), nick-naming my brother after Edward Albee:
where has it brought me?
to the edge of the story – infinity

the haze
the bafflement of (youthful) age

Nov 2011

Label and Destroy

Everything possible to be believ'd is an image of truth
– from "The Marriage of Heaven & Hell" by William
Blake

How can you tell me what Light *really is*?
by describing it as chemistry?
no one really knows what Light is…
it wasn't made by man

unless you believe in the Christian myth,
the same might be said of Love
(I would not *send out the raven ahead of the dove*)

light is a magic substance
that floods the universe
makes stars sparkle, fills days
floods lamps
enters beings
lifts souls
keeps out the damp

more than heat, it's fairy dust;
as fire, it does a dance;

Love's a similar mystery
a substance we know not from whence

and while, like light, it sometimes fades,
it can create a trance
transmogrify the world
travel through flesh
or light-reflecting eyes
or (when helping someone
in disgrace with fortune and men's eyes)*
save a life
transport a soul to heaven
see through all disguise;

no one really knows the Source
of Light, of Love, of Truth
you might well say the Sun or Heart
but those are mysteries, too,

not invented by man.

November 29, 2008

*Shakespeare's Sonnet XXIX

Bella Luna

The moon shimmers in green water
while herons fly through the moonlight.

The young man hears a girl gathering water-chestnuts;
Into the night, singing, they paddle home together –
"Autumn River Song" by Li Po

beautiful pale moon; tonight you are bursting your seams!
as if, like those you represent, you are trying to break through old structures,
protocols, laws, principles, the walls of history,
the patterns of universal design itself!
as though you've been besieged for too long and would rip open
and out would spew a torrent of temper, fumes of fury,
a wrathful rage!

Bella Luna, full, white, round as breasts,
how do you awaken the beast yet tame him at the same time?
Guardian of girls, you help things grow in a quiet, feminine way,
slowly, assuredly, under cover of darkness

we know, too, that you are home for the Rabbit

who constantly pounds herbs for the Immortals,
though Li Po says it's in vain

Why? Perhaps because the Immortals are sick from
how we've treated their mother –
Gaia; Isis is weeping for her;
our destruction has made her too ill for herbs to heal
her

and yet we should thank the busy Jade Rabbit
because the moon still *shimmers in green water*
in some places
and a few *herons* still *fly through the moonlight,*
once in a while,

though only the truly fortunate actually see them now

Vancouver & Tasmania, March 2011

About Time

tick tick
here comes the poem
about time
the true god

that illusive dominatrix
in the background
who keeps coming
knocking at our door

slinking like the silent predator
it has become
the disciplinarian at first
who then becomes a
kind of fun friend

that later morphs into
a kind of teacher's bet
a grandparent
warning you to use it wisely
cherish it
like a beloved pet

nurture it
or it shall leave you
on someone else's doorstep

scratching your eyes
wondering where it went

the lonely hunter
of the essence
whom you let go
a-squandering
in the late fields
of Alti-land

nurture it
or it shall leave you
abandoned
forever

Aug. 12, 2019

Lines for a Poem about Earthly Demise

funny little baby face of death

her little pagan voice
trying to be heard above the din
of dogmatic self-righteous
self-appointed dowagers and doges

only wanting to go back to her homeland
without all the fuss and frippery

long before gods, and even goddesses, appeared,
back to her home among the stones

and plants and trees and mushrooms
a new kind of throne

among her sisters and brothers
heretofore unknown

spirits can move in mysterious ways
and no one knows from whence we came

or where we alight

so, goodnight, little sprite,
feel bright!

goodnight…

June 4, 2018

The Will

I will
sleep in the makeshift morning,
shine in the working afternoon,
swim in the early evening
and gleam in the black shiny dark

I will
meet the king of bees in the red yellow garden
of love with peonies twined
in my naughty mane

I will
raise a brood of violets, memories and regrets
in the dusty woods of winter
and the orchestra of orchids will praise hell

I will
dance to symphonies of sadness
and tear off my drowsy dress
in fields of tears floating down like silver notes
in the midnight blue evening air
moon on sky

I will
waste the Saturdays of solitude
watching films about obsessive love

and damaging passions that wrench the
battered walls of the heart's caverns

I will
watch for you day and night, wait for
your silhouette on the haunted highway of dreams
where a woman sweeps lilies off the veranda
and rocks and rocks in her butterfly chair

until the moment of arrival – the oil lamp flickering in
the breeze.

I will

Look for you in the hidden forest of words
and broken pictures, on the stage, in the backrooms,
on the shiny boardwalks and boozy battleground bars –
the perilous paths of pain,

among the angelfish and orangutans,
the tangled oceans and the light

look for me

I will
wait…

I will –

(circa 1994)

Chariot – for Maxie

*Charity suffereth long, and is kind; charity envieth not;
...vaunteth not itself, is not puffed up, / Doth not
behave itself unseemly, seeketh not her own, is not
easily provoked, thinketh no evil;/ Rejoiceth not in
iniquity, but rejoiceth in the truth;/ Beareth all things,
believeth all things, hopeth all things, endureth all
things.* 1 Corinthians 13:4-7

You're my chariot, my horse, my wings
you take me up up up to the highest things
heights of fancy lit up by the moon

you're my Spoon
who dishes out all the feasts, roast beast
(poor little lambs gone astray
little black sheep lost their way)
*into the tray go the hundred thousand
how have they fallen!*

you are kind – generous to a fault line
give quietly like a monk in a wood
offer whatever's needed, wordlessly

you envy not; are not puffed up
except by snowburn on a mountain crag
shining exploits of which you never brag

not easily provoked, you take us all in stride
your giant step ranges across all divides

you bear all things
nobly, like a white horse
a chariot
with wings –

Aug. 2012

We Gods

I'm half deity, half dust – Lord Byron.

Maybe we are actual flesh and blood deities like the Greeks and Pagans talked about… one foot in the metaphor for heaven one lodged deep in that made-up hell; straddling giants, vulnerable to love and selfishness, struggling to climb out of the mud of muddledness; holy vegetable and mineral, electrical – a dash of stardust sprinkled in – and animal, the difficult part, the beast with his yearnings; and then, of course, there's the reptile, the fight and flight instinct part of a god that makes wars, headed for extinction; but still, we walk in beauty, masters of all we convey, minds mighty as computers, gods with hearts in disarray, loving, hurt, creative, forged in Blake's holy fire, a mystery from somewhere unknown seated at our own earthly altars, reaching for the stars, trying to get home

May, 2009

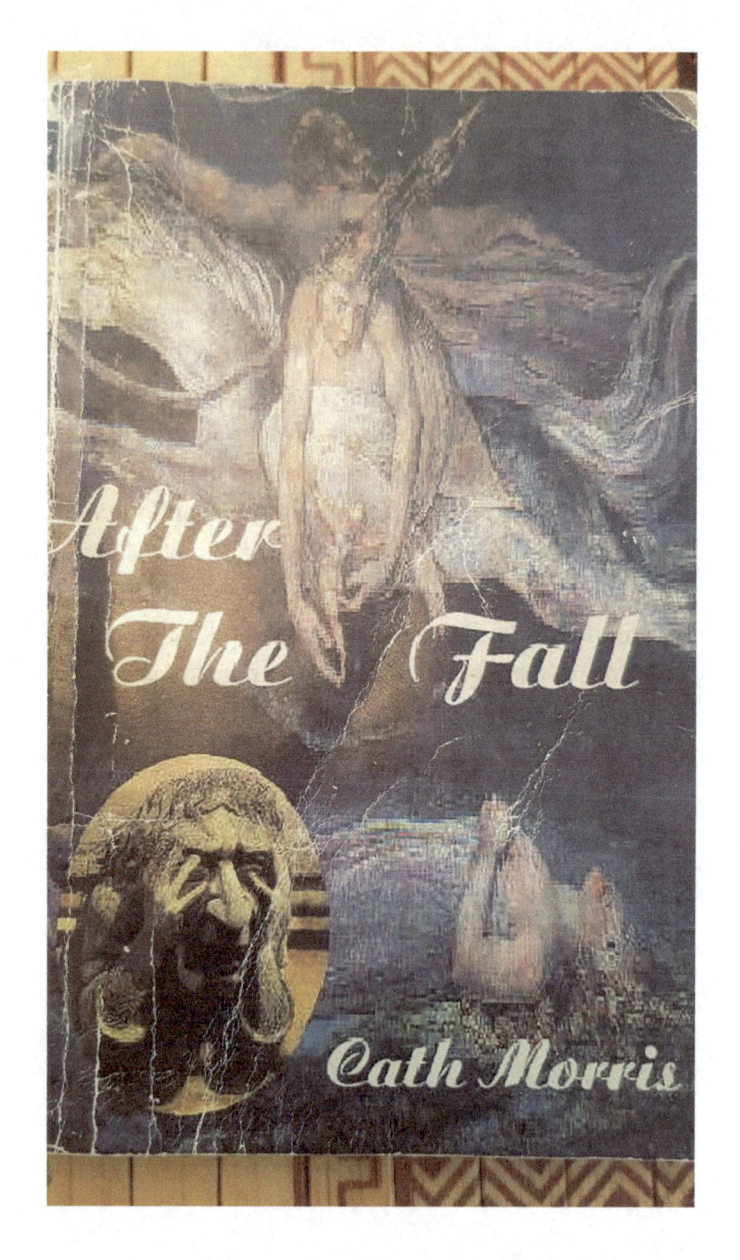

After The Fall

Cath Morris

PART TWO

Man did not weave the web of life – he is merely a strand in it.
Whatever he does to the web, he does to himself.
Chief Seattle, 1854.

Editorial Assistance from George Stanley
and Bob Waukulich

Cover Art: collage with *Pity* by William Blake and front cover photo of Oxford Gargoyle by Thomas Photos – Oxford.
Back cover: portion of photo by E.S. Curtis, 1914.

Cover concept by author.
Book designed by Max Cutcliffe.

Interior native drawings of frog and bird by Croft Faircrest. The author owns them.

Photo of the author (back cover) taken by Jack Williams

After the Fall

He who binds to himself a Joy Doth the winged life
destroy; But he who kisses the joy as it flies
Lives in Eternity's sunrise.*

I
The conquering races are falling down like skyscrapers
at a Wrecker's Ball;
they scraped the sky 'til there were giant holes
in the old blue wind
where spirits once roamed like oxygen

(Two men walk into a bar – "Hey, man, this place has
no atmosphere")
brittle shells of white intruders, lost and hollow-eyed
in bars,
like eggs now empty of their meat – fragile but
hardened

drinking money that became God and wondering
where God went,
what to do for their redemption;
falling…

they forgot what they drink to remember
and in the morning
remember what they drank to forget –

now there are machines to remember for them,
shredding memories of fire, dance, hearth, mask,
gods of all kinds.
The ceremonies of innocence are drowned

II

Where will they go now, these pale-faced men,
home to their single wasp-hive cells –
to cybergirls and cyberdogs,
when they finally find – like Columbus off course –
no fleshly women left to walk beside
(another out of favour commodity on the exchange)
caught in the necromantic net of money,
cars and condo-castles.

The conquering races are dancing an unsteady jig
to the heavy-metal honky noise of modern city night,
like lonesome tumbling towers – crumbling
as the comforting drumbeats of innocent ceremony
retreat into the last patch of wilderness
untouched by the overwhelming sea of flotsam
falling…

away from the four directions, ignoring the muffled
warnings of the elders:
water (floods), earth (quakes), air (ozone), fire
(blazes);

that's the only way elements can talk.
Do microchips remember the cathartic rapture of ritual,
the consolation of community, the wisdom of family,
the masks behind the masks?
The village square? The thought behind the word?
This is not a rehearsal.

III

"Turning and tuning in the widening gyre"
the falconer can no longer hear the falcon –
things are getting clogged in the cogs

as they turn and gouge
and regurgitate the endless productions of consumer
gods.

We were almost there –
then stared too long at statues,
crouched too long in Descartes' lair
sat so long in the tenured chairs of reason –
something changed

IV

And I looked out the window
heard the constant whine of cars,
the moan of buses in the downpour,
heard the sirens, smelled the gasses, saw the people
rushing to and fro – running somewhere to do
something, anything –
hearts beating out their painful rhythms
under overcoats and hats and approaching snow

tiny strings of time and space, a noodle universe,
following chaotic rhythms that may have nothing to do
with thought…. or everything…

branches, veins, the skeletons of leaves, the ratios of
growth – speak of order –

just a small group of fractally-patterned limbs in the
infinitesimal gigantic dance
of carbon and stars and stiletto ghetto boys –

and micro men in the macro world follow along the
same tributaries as these mathematical highways,
not noticing.

One must keep a watchful eye on clocks, bars,
patterns, selfish time and synchronicities,

on rain-drenched streets of sound

the searching eyes of animals around us
on all connecting tissue, sinews, tribes of
consciousness,

and after the fall is over, after the falling away,
we must remember to remember the patterns of frailty,
the salt-sea blood in everything, the kind white blood
of trees, the supra-silicon connections behind eyes of
any shape and the universal music of
falling...

and I will try not to grieve the growing power of the
robot reign

He Who Binds to Himself – by William Blake

The Drowning Sea

The wind was high on the jazzy sea
currents coursing through the up and down
and the wind was blowing right through me
on that Maxfield Parrish sundown at the sea.

I fought through those cut-diamond waves
like a dolphin-knife, a missionary,
feeling the salt-spray at my heels
letting the water caress me, embrace me,

(for I was sorely in need of a hug that night);
now supporting, now slapping my face,
like a jealous mistress in a rage,
now pouncing like a tiger, this foaming mother.

The seals followed me all along my route,
their big eyes wide and wet with calm concern,
for they seemed to love me then, I felt,
and thought that I was one of them.

Now as I lie on my bed, far away from anything blue except me,
a strange desire sweeps over my soul –
to let my spirit dissolve, like salt in water,

into the great living soul of All That Is,
the earth, the sun, the stars, the moon and trees,
but above all to merge with the jazzy, drowning sea.

July 1996

Star Moths

(in memoriam for Michel Delaunay)

You're crazed; you fly, like a wounded buffalo moth,
head first into the light
where your madness is sharpened and finalized.

You're the swooning poet of the painting
splayed on the loveseat under the windowed moon
your red velvet waistcoat hanging limply on the chair,
scraps of tattered paper strewn like rose petals
everywhere.

Why choose the Pre-Raphaelite agonies and postures?

On this cool, clear October night
as I lie here on the Sechelt Peninsula
watching the night sky,
the upside-down stars remind me of the spark circuit
that is your Mozart-infused mind;

and how you told me precisely what he was thinking
in every segment
of each allegro;

these stars remind me of the astounding order found in
randomness,

of all the women you've shown those big bear teeth to,
that licorice leer that throws them off guard
and makes them more vulnerable
to your cultivated advances;

of the unfathomable number of possibilities,
the intersecting fates of lovers,
and ultimately,
the excruciating uniqueness of each person's path.

This evening on the sound,
when the salmon-gold sunset bathed the mountains in
such a holy, eerie light
they came alive, like big soft brothers.

I am crazed.
I fly, like a gypsy moth,
head first into your light.

copyright October 1991

Monopoly

...and after that the crumbling of the moon,
the soul remembering its loneliness
shudders in many cradles. – from *The Phases of the*
Moon (Wild Swans at Coole) – William Butler Yeats

Here comes the crumbling of the moon;
like the bulb that's been held in the hand too long,
in the central office of the new sidereal real estate…

Stars for sale! Get your own personal piece of the
heavens right here!
Name a star after your newborn babe!

In musical chairs, the chaos of turbulence slowly
gathers
And someone's always left without a chair
Until the last man sits triumphant all alone,
mid-world,
while the other players begin to disperse
drifting away to some new contest,
where, once again, they hope to win
or acquire something.

Stars for sale!

Imagine – eternity for only a hundred dollars –

immortality for a song –

I've got your song right here:

I've got your star right here, his name is Upper Sphere,
and he can guarantee the time of year,
can do, candu, this guy says the star can do…

And the Little Red Hen is crying,
while the Trolls snicker under the bridge
in the dark, dark waters of the greedy river
(somewhere down the greedy river)

and a few guys have all the hotels
and Marvin Gardens, Boardwalk and Park Place,
and someone's sitting all alone
when the game is over,
on the sacred tree of property
whispering:

Stars for sale… don't be frail
Get your shiny new stars over here…
As he watches the moon crumbling
In the much too busy sky.

January 1996

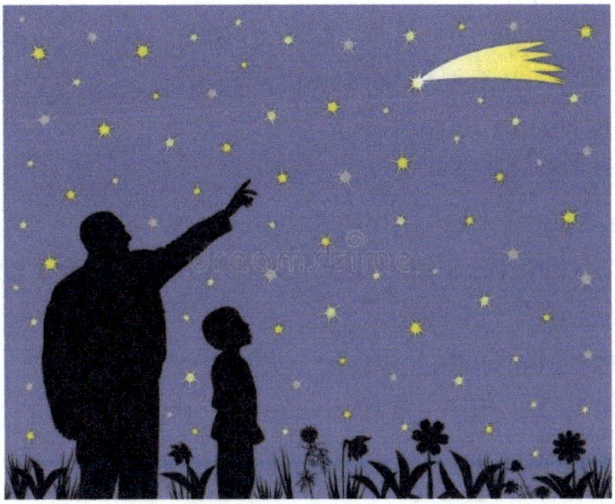

Cleopatra in The Big Shop of Horrors

(for my beautiful mother)

Haven't been seeing things too clearly lately
(like Vancouver slithering in the rain through a bus window,
splotchy images behind the condensation –
blurred lights through hand-smudged peepholes)
the way truth is –
blurred
and whizzing by too fast.

The surprise of beauty comes
like the raindrop web the small sidewalk tree becomes…
in front of the streetlamp;
the closer you get
the more the twiggy branches form the illusion
of concentric configuration
with the light at its center –

like the unexpected moments of serenity
in the hospital room
where mother is graciously weaving
her own delicate web of death

taking her leave – like a faded Cleopatra

on her way to meet the Anthony that was my young
father, is my dead father –
(though near the end she said she saw him in a vision
as a young Highlander on a hill)
after the sudden silent sting of the small serpent
that represents the tumor
of self-propelled departure –
grotesque inside her pretty mouth.

This is a fast serpent –
all the unexpressed nos of her life
having lain in wait to form this alien "Audrey"
from the BIG SHOP OF HORRORS
and yet, the courage and grace she bestowed,
conquering-queen-like, on all she met,
all who entered this sterile room,
still fills the final stage
like soft perfume.

Her eyes have no fear in them
(like some dying bishops' have)
but if you look closely
you can see a thin veil of condensation over them

like on bus windows in the rain.

April 1997

Motorless Replicant

maybe it's true
that we're nothing but cleverly programmed
giant flesh and bone robots

sometimes I feel like a motorless replicant
sometimes I feel like a motorless replicant

and each one is set for a specified few years
with built-in desires and emotions –
a body flying into the river –
a severed arm off on its own –
and a good working mechanism for tears –

but we have composite blood
some other supra-galactic origins mixed in:

sometimes I feel like a motorless replicant
sometimes I feel like a motorless replicant
sometimes I feel like a motorless replicant
a long long way from Home

I hope it's true, Mr. Tyrell,
'cause I'd like an operation if it's so
you can snip the wires around the heart
and set it free – like a crushed bird module –

you made us too well, Mr. Tyrell,
geneticist, snake Charmer, Devil, Witch
you tinkered with some tender toys
and some of the wires have got loose

it's that persistent memory of two moons
I can't shake
and we sang like glass harmonicas in a high-pitched wail
like heart-broken tin men in a field of monkeys…

it's that notion of a sublime, infinitely old,
infinitely wise race
that shook off its shackles millennia ago
I can't shake

and it's the high-pitched dancing of giant soft robots
in the double-helix moonlight
round a great sparkling fire
against an infinite night…

sometimes I feel like a motorless replicant
a long, long way from my star.

1994 *

* This poem was published in *Cascadia: Make it True*, Leaf Press, April 30, 2015

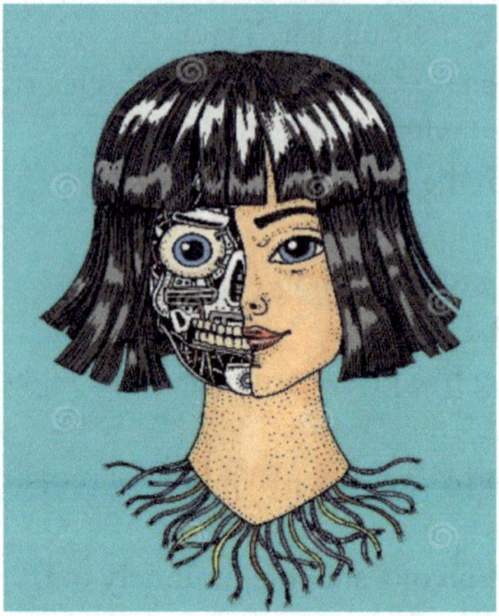

Red Donkeys

These are the years piling up on you
like red donkeys
these are the tears that fill the room;
standing water must be examined
before anything like consummation can be performed.

These are the Friday afternoons of empty sunlight
closing around you like a giant airy vice
The Battle of Rejection was lost
for the want of a wayward spike.

What the hell is going on here, Mister?
These are the days you go home to your 'wife'.

What of afternoons on the boulevard
the arm-in-arm stroll of calm delight?
What of the slapping of thighs
like lapping waves, you said,
and all of those up-too-late nights?

the tossing of words on a table,
the mumbling of words in an ear
what of the humming of foghorns as bodies vibrate
together – like Ishmael holding his spear.

The years are merely red donkeys

neighing and whinnying so –
these are the doppelganger parties
of split-soul unheavenly hosts

I merely wish to understand, my quiet stray,
how you can be in two places at once
as the moon howls down on my face,
and why the years are red donkeys
and someone's waiting, always waiting
to take my place in the standing water
waiting to step into my space.

1996

Long Moons

(after hearing Neil Eustache read at Blacksheep Books, Vancouver)

it's the short staccato monologues like fast edit much music movie slipstream
crying out the raw pain of every felt moment of movement toward and movement away they want, is it? You sweet native son you quiet suffering lyric punk of a poet, speak a little louder so more people can hear your war cry and tears falling inside – the canyons of your struggling soul so vast and tender – I have reservations about your quiet scream while the world dances around you so noisily and just because we're alienated and fragmented, disconnected, overloading and exploding, building 'em taller and higher and progress at any cost (effective) and tearing it down like a tinker-toy tree-town forest rape, moan, groan, doesn't mean we don't care... O stop and save us – reconnect us to the roots we've so systematically cut so we can climb back up and branch out properly – more beautifully connected to sky, sun, sea, earth, air, whatever's left when they're through... can we get through to the light? Do we need you to send us the Star People again to show us where we went astray? Where are the people 'lowered from whence' now? Ashinabe. Forgive us for we knew not the extent of the

technopath of destruct… We got greedy and grew like
a giant machine that gathers weight like a snowball as
it rolls – down to the Precipice of Avarice where it
totters on the verge of the Valley of Decision, waiting
for instructions from Mic Mac Blo… There is some
vague ancient ancestral memory
of at-home-in-the-jungle-LOVE and life in harmonious
earth-embrace with outdoor clean water earth tree odor
air – and rocks that talk with birds and us, too… happy
for a soft split-second of truth remembering the here-
and-now-time of life-on-Earth… long moons ago.

1996

Wolf Courses

the secret garden is near laid bare; it has been found
out, explored
by the wolves who stretch themselves across the world
ever seeking more space in which to devour and play
(more wolf courses for playing with sticks)
more world in which to plant their terrible claws, and
nothing else –
nothing to replace it with

the wolves in suits who scuttle and devour
and tease a tree 'til nothing more remains, and work
the ground 'til no one can live in it – take their
mangled prey and go home again
laying it at the feet of corporate mates, and wait;

lounging until the next hunt – on beds of nails, to
heighten character,
to bolster dead spirits in luxurious retreats,

until the table once again is set with meats;

the conversation takes its course,
(*of such sweet breath composed*)

seeking consciences no longer there, arousing this
one's desire and that one's insouciant glare – 'til,
weary from the kill they climb to duvet-covered lairs

the secret garden has no more place to hide and little
grows there anymore;

ivy, rhododendron, and medicinal blooms are clawed
from earthy beds already stripped – of canopies and
shade and oxygen

while wolves of industry paw and scratch across the
world
fingering and sniffing round the table, where rock stars
and ecologists dine
among the linen and the silverware.

O the little miniatures remain: secret tracts of wall-
protected green

But these wolves have become tool-users, routers,
arsonists,
And fire burns satin petticoats as well as bugs and
leaves.

July 1997

Fantasy

In a white brushed-cotton dress she surveys the
evening crowd, lounging under canopies whiter yet,
themselves in turn, lounging under stars, also faintly
white. The rest is yellow black and midnight blue,
tonight out in the air, wine glasses shined up by the
moon; waiting for the Carnival to commence. Distant
strums purl on the air, mingle with the murmuring
men... candlelight on the hair makes it shimmer, in the
dark night air, not yet cool. Someone knocks over a
stool. The waiter grins and sets it right, tonight, in the
fragrant air. Music approaches in snatches, like wafts
of hapless breeze. Now soft drums, now tambourine,
now guitar and cymbals... and the accordion washes
in, like the sound of a rocking river. The heart forgets
everything and smiles. As musicians emerge from the
dark street, so also masked revelers follow close
behind already lifting their feet and swaying back and
forth to the celebratory tune that floats on the evening
air, so warm, so inviting, so cruel. Tonight. Here now a
prancing cat with long black paws and lashes its large
feline breasts bouncing up and down in time, its
whiskers perfumed and pert. The favourite, Arlequino,
rouses choruses of applause, his ambulation agile as a
diamond-checkered horse, his artful antics dazzling
and familiar as remorse... Another well-beloved face

appears, the huge head bobbing to and fro; it smiles that thousand-year-old smile frozen in lacquered clay (so we can see it today) – the jolly Buddha lumbers forth… and in his hand the sacred cow with mechanical head that turns and bobs on a pivotal spring, the eyes alight in electric red from some device placed under the head… Now the snake charmer, now Lili Marlene, not two paces behind, Astaire and Rogers, Dracula and several dwarves besides bring up the rear. Here the Seven Sisters come, twisting 'neath their flowing robes in orgiastic ecstasy, re-enacting the old rites, in homage to the great Baal, god of festivals. In hot pursuit, brandishing a long whip of feathers, the Marquis de Sade struts like a dandified cock, satanic grin perfected under powdered wig, the scent of brothel mixed with talc emanating from his body like ribbons of air, in the dastardly cool night windless breeze on the streets of Carnival Time.

Endless numbers of creatures appear, the next more garish than the last: thespian initiates, glamorous compatriots, blasphemous ventriloquists, satirical deliricists, until the street throbs with mirth and mystery… The Carnival's begun, the wine floats in mid-air, the laughing air, tonight, the cool night air.

The girl in the white brushed-cotton dress makes up her mind. She is pleased. Tonight she will dance only with strangers.

October 1982

When We Were Fish

(a love poem to someone I thought was dying) (for RMW)

I want to take you past time to the beautiful blue beyond
where the living architecture breathes and grows in the swaying void

I want
to shed the flesh – be more embryonic –
like a gecko girl – pure and transparent
in order to love you from spirit to post
as young lizards love
mentally – quietly – thoughtfully,
rarely blinking

to show you the breath of the forest
as it exhales the mystery of its ancient being –
tread on its delicate skeletal floor
crackling with the joy of decay
echoing the sparks of stars.

to stumble on pebbles and logs with you
get lost in the living geometry of patterns
let the colours resonate
and whisper

their intimate music in the twilight

to polish sea-rounded stones with watery hands
feel the smooth of the curves and the rough of living
rock,

bask in the softening orange light, like tired seals,
sit with you and wait for the moon…

to wade into the sea with you

immerse ourselves in her giant salt womb
let her lift us like balloons
reminding us of the primordial time
when we were fish.

October 1997

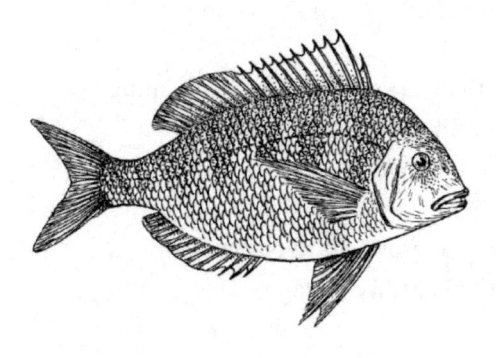

Cobalt Blue – for Jack Williams

In July, the river Styx is a glittering meadow
of cobalt blue
and the hunchback heron on the water raft
knows how to silhouette himself precisely against the
salmon-red sunset

It is a good month to die in, Jack

but life is always too short
especially for those left on shore

I can feel you pulling back the reins of Charon's
chariot
(that wily Chess Player who moves the king into
position when the whim takes Him)

he is cool, collected – lights a cigarette with you,
almost in unison – or on the same match

I feel the thick cord between us stretching
into a fine silk thread that's fraying
and about to break –

as you prepare yourself to embark,
on your final earthly voyage –

gathering your loved ones around you
as if they were logs you were arranging in a boom,
or cargo you wanted to take with you
I can only stand on the shoreline

staring helplessly out at the cobalt blue
watching the crazy boat grow smaller and smaller on the horizon,
waving my fading faint farewell

Belle voyage, my friend who was so good at living;
show that wily Chess Player what you're made of –

what He doesn't know is that
you were always several moves ahead of the rest of us.

July 1997

Winter Rain

the seagulls are crying in the besotted breeze
winter rain groans on like a woman who can't stop
weeping, no safety valve in her tear duct chamber.
They remind me of the tears of Ariadne when she
awakes to find Theseus has abandoned her on the blue
island shores of Dia – and no Dionysius to take his
place; or those of her mother, Pasiphae, whose
unnatural passions gave birth to Minos, father of the
Minotaur, the unfortunate beast whom Ariadne, her
daughter, plotted with Theseus to slaughter, using her
trick with thread.
I, too, must find the unbreakable thread that will lead
to the heart of this Labyrinthine life and murder the
beast within – in order to stop this incessant rain.
My only husband – I am diminished by your death.
Your unrelenting absence (as I stare at my overly
made-up face in the fading mirror) is palpable, and I
am somehow less a woman without you in the world –
no matter where you may have sometimes been.

And like Pasiphae, I must tame the passions that claw
at my soul as the city sputters and belches beneath my
lonely balcony in the last gasping snorts of Poseidon's
wrath that are

January in Vancouver.   - January 1998

The Olive: An Ode

the olive is a black mild tree fruit when ripe
with a texture like the tougher form of mushroom
or the human heart

it is what we call central, that is, basic, core,
or quintessential
with many of the tightly-packed characteristics of the
seed
and a sense of its own importance

a marvel of nature, like the egg, or the kiss
it cries out – yet gives all –
reminiscent of a sexy thing,
the dark flesh having such a subtle taste –
the acquired taste, we might say, of forbidden fruit;

the olive is a black mild fruit of the tree,
Olea Europaea,
ancient – and therefore wise –
with the power to heal and the power to corrupt

its wilful branches have inspired man to art
and its nectar tempts virgin nymphs from their unholy
state

the mere whiff of its perfume can cause to salivate,
lasciviously,
the most fastidious of chefs…

in brief, it resembles the apple of Eden

in its possession of magic power and symbolic stature

while maintaining an innocence beyond measure or
reproach
like the Earth herself
or some other celestial being
before its fall.

1995

Four West Coat Haikus

lantern light on brick
obscured by red ivy fading:
hotel by the sea

heron on old log:
when I move, where do you go?
with you goes the morning

in the machine age
robot-people fear to cry for rusting –
how sad!

in this darkened glade
sunlight slides between the trees
white, black, like early films

20th century/ 1997

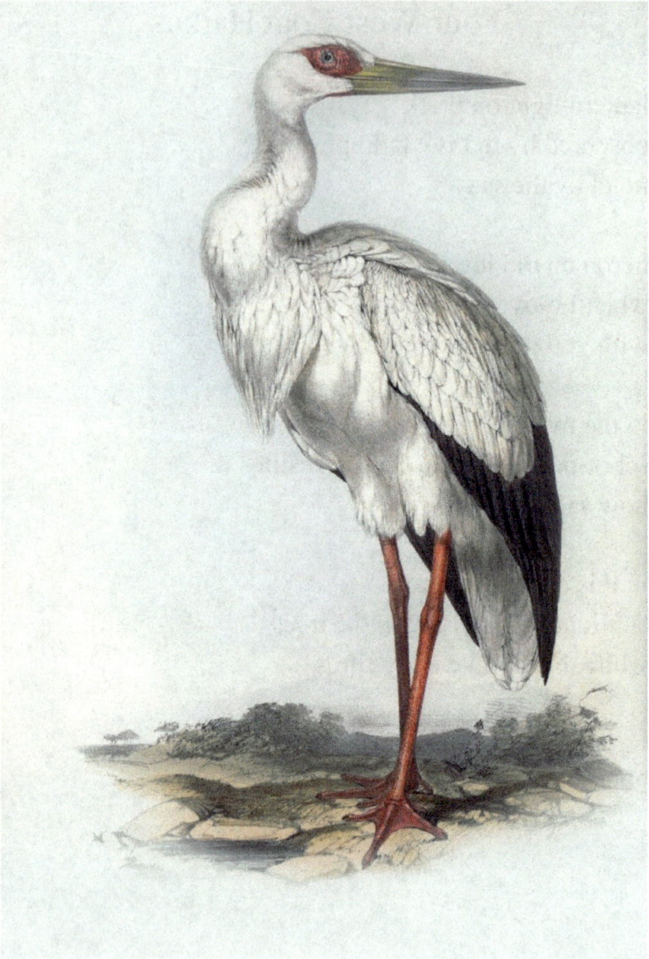

Experiments with Sonnets

(to a Russian poet-critic and friend)

A The world of Non-Pandemos is a cup
B wherein I would be drowned in the froth
A had not I such a friend to pick me up
B and teach me ways to counteract my sloth
B and so, my sullen master, I bow down
C and drink to your superior skill
B and hope that in the cup I do not drown
C await instructions and curtsy to your will
C and hope that some turned phrase produce a thrill
D so please go easy on a trembling soul
C who wishes but to please you and to fill
D that cup from which you drink; I'll be a mole
E who burrows furiously into books
E and sighs and screeches with the learned rooks.

July 1997

An Artist's Dream

The horses of Delacroix are tired.
Their massive flanks lie twitching on the ground.
Their eyes plead with dumb wonder.
Agony of Life, what is your business?

There's a sinking raft in the picture,
caught by a massive wave;
Bodies twisted in the growling water's thrust;
oh agony, you are an artist's dream!

What catches my eye! Black crows in a field of yellow
corn,
the sky aswirl in an anguished mind,
the sun hotter and golder than a human heart
can bear.

Here's a girl in long robes waiting, writing a lonely
letter at her morning desk. Solitude shines through the
deep long windows in streaks of cruel white light.
Agony of life. Teach us your dark purpose.

You are the sullen mistress of days and hours, the
eccentric twin sister of death, the messenger of lost
love and tragic news, wearing a torn dark dress

I'll fight you like a lady, whisper you away from my door, banish your cunning with laughter. O Agony of Life, you shall not outwit me.

For I have colours to console me; light, shadow, chiaroscuro, and fingers to tap my pain out, and dreams to brush the mind with

I have the massage of media and the super-graduated senses of touch, smell, vision, hearing, breath, taste, god.

I am an artist's dream.

April 1995

The Ride

can't believe we're really riding the tail end of the wave
like Slim Pickens on the nuclear bronco
heading for the final blowout

that we're handing the kids this battered old Earth
like a tar-covered tennis ball,
saying, "Here's your future; make the best of it."

play on play on
play on the Babylon bubble

play on the last stretch of beach
make castles in the murky air

if you can find any space between the gasping whales
and the moonlit oil on the rocks

oozing from the heart of the machine.

April 1998

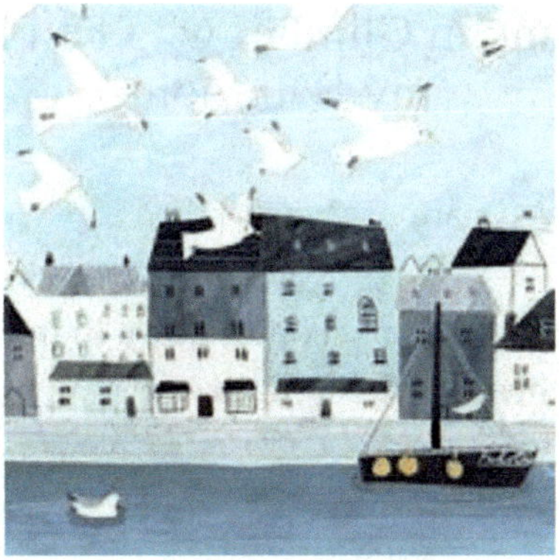

The Mountain Climber who Fell Down in my Bathroom

for my beloved partner, Max

The mountain climber who fell down in my bathroom
bumped his head on the toilet-paper dispenser

he's okay now

but nothing's been the same since then…

for awhile he looked like Gorbachev
with a dark red map of Mount McKinley on his
forehead

lately he's been trying to negotiate the mountain of me
from his married aerie,

poor fellow
I'm so steep and treacherous

he might have better luck with the arêtes of Patagonia

or wrestling the snow leopard
on a glacial ridge

he's down there now, skirting the edges of mood volcanoes...

and my toilet-paper dispenser still sits neglected on the wicker hamper
waiting to be mounted.

March 1998

A Pecunious Woman is a Harloty thing
(a blues song)

by any other name – she must play
play up or pay

piping wild in catacombs of humble hunger

but sweet soul can never be defiled

humility can extract sweetness
like plump plums in a gender-blender

or elder berries in a still (life)

a pecunious woman can lose her nerve

prostrating before the masculine monolithic bullion
like a fakir at Mecca

despite fair bosom and dangling hair
it hides like a pink petunia in a rock garden
scanning the sky for blue ships

or, like a pheasant under smoky glass
waits decorously – to be devoured

grinning like a butterfly

bowing like a vine
playing possum like a she-bear
lying like a harlot in a welfare line

it's a kind of penury.

May 1998

The River

the urgent rush of the Nooksack –
this tumbling turquoise message from the melting
mountain
becomes its veins
speaks the rage of ages (with a solemn joy)

gushes over and down and through
the rocky bed
on its way forever to nowhere –
fills me,
makes the river of my blood flow
insistently, inevitably,

while the long-fallen crisscrossed firs and cedars
along the bed
practise the geometry of woods, rocks and water,
deep blue-green spirits dance beneath its
rough surface

it rises up in crests,
like small white mountains of consciousness
on green blown-glass

remembering something
mysterious
we've long forgotten…

we are silenced
by the strange white roar

of its turbulent music

insistent and unfathomable as time.

May 1998

Postmodern Crow

Poised on the streetlamp, the gleaming black crow
surveys his city kingdom like a sentinel,
watches the strange peregrinations of cars and people
below –
as they drop a piece of bread here, a milk carton there,
unwittingly feeding his dark hunger...

there are sounds: a woman crying, a child screaming,
cars whizzing, sirens wailing

Is watching this scene as stimulating for him as
perusing the beach?
Is he amused, amazed, disgusted, tired, bored?
How long has this trickster been recording our history
with his black eyes?

How does the noise affect him?

As the yellow and blue days grow longer,
the sounds of street life get louder,
until the whizzing buzzing street teems with voracious
humanity –
young men sitting in sidewalk cafes, imbibing,
hooting at the top of their voices to prove their
manliness (little knowing it has the opposite effect)

back and forth go the wandering shells, ever seeking
the diversion that works:
shopping, eating, gulping, watching, driving, riding,
surfing (net); taking the dog for a stroll;
always doing – running, hiding, something, anything
to get out from under the steady gaze of the Big Black
Crow

who stares indifferently down on them all,
vigilantly registering the accelerating story
of this strange restless species
on the videotape of his shining black eyes

waiting…

June 1997

Adamantine

You are glass –
hard, reflective, cool
and your thoughts rise like mountain arêtes
from a crystalline pool –

thoughts are things – or become so
at the point of emergence into form
they bloom into floral realities
and make their effects in the world

some thoughts shine
like jewels
green, red, blue,
some are more like tumors
growing inside the head – these must be battled
as dragons,
brought to bear, taught to submit, be subdued,
loved away, perhaps,
faced, certainly, recognized, acknowledged,
taken to task – put to bed, but not buried.

Thoughts can be wishes
or dreams –
inventions of the most spectacular kind!
cobalt birds,
towers,

chrysanthemums,
milk-bowls,
lists –
poems.

I treasure your clear blue thoughts
and sunny ways
(the way they ascend to the heights
of days)

they gleam.
like glass,
even though
adamantine.

Octobruary 1998

Wakener
(to the great Haida artist, Bill Reid)

Ancient sculptor, genius, creator…

your Bear Mother broke out of the amniotic gold
like a fish leaping out of mercury
to suckle her cubs openly,
the human teats pulled by hungry infant bear teeth,
revealing at once the stubborn pain of motherhood
and the golden gleaming joy of it.

Schoolmaster…
you went around to all the sleeping beds of two cultures
and gently lifted eyelids (white and red) by the eyelashes,
leading us into the light
where we began to see, through your objects,
with our hearts.

Flame-tender…
you breathed your fiery breath on the last embers of a dying culture
and built a bonfire of souls
that towered above the rest.

Guardian of ancient arts,

you created new monoliths out of old
that stood high enough for all to notice,
forcing the world to sit up, look,
and try to understand.

Bridge-builder…
your small objects
(silver creatures, golden eagles, spirit frogs)

spanned centuries and cultures –
from the old in the new
to the new of the old –
spoke quietly their ancient language
just sitting on a table or in a museum shop.

Gulliver…
giant among faces
and dweller among the tiny,
you invited us into the secret world of the miniature,
that you knew contained everything.

You awakened dying spirits
to view themselves anew,
through the brilliant mirror of your skill,
emancipating our animal ancestors from jade-glazed bronze,
(vigorously jostling for space in the crowded black
canoe: life-raft: the Earth)

on the sea of humanity,
to remind us of our brotherhood,
and teach us what your Haida brethren have known for centuries
about the mystery and the universal message
contained in u-forms, ovoids, and s-curves.

Boat-builder,
your canoe barged through the hallowed heavy doors
of the halls of European Anthropology
(without apology)
in the cultural center of the conquering empire
that held stolen dead samples of your once-living art

and turned the structure of western academe on its head.

You saw the faces in all natural objects
from all archipelagos
and freed them from the enslavement
of old wood
and the bigotry of wooden ideas.

I build this little fire
as a monument
to your great spirit
and dance around it
singing

to the ancient rhythms you
taught us
about the life in things.

January 1999

A Clump of Monks

A clump of monks sat under the baobab tree,
quietly mortar-and-pestling their crystallized souls into
a soft white powder that,
when added sparingly,
can pique the flavour of any evening vesper stew.

They sat
like a slaughter of crows
on their several perches, so picturesquely random,
so adjacent, complacent, curiously bored

they bore down hard on the Holy Spirit
for fear of falling into pholepsies* so exquisite
no civil servant or engineer could possibly understand
or render them on any parchment
nor even the most accomplished scribe illuminate
them…

when shining shafts of morning ran like swords
through their transparent torsos,
their long robes flowed and folded like melting
chocolate
on cold bronze statues…

contemplating the Holy Virgin
took feats of skill and meditative practice

many of them lacked
as their thoughts drifted much more easily,
to other, more masculine, mortal pursuits…
often only the long gold sound of the giant gong at dawn
could wake them from these orgiastic reveries…

it was then they drank penance like mulled wine
and huddled in small clumps on dusty stone floors
like a cluster of mushrooms
or a flock of starlings who all wake up from the same dream
at the same time – and flutter off to the next convention
or riverbank…

here they settle down to eat their rice and flaxseed
(keeps them regular)
and green grapes in red clay bowls,
homemade potato bread, no butter..

later, after digging deep and planting their seedling
supplications in the spiritual garden
they busy themselves translating ancient crumbling
manuscripts for the visiting abbots,
or cultivating purity and transitoriness
contemplating air and roots,
standing rapt like tender saplings in a tall wood…

chanting diligently to keep the metropolis at bay
(with its sweet temptations)
ever keeping their eye on the ultimate prize –
that branch on the cliffside that must be reached for
when one is falling, even in clumps…

* pholepsy – a rapt state induced by craving for the unattainable

Fulfillment

To look past balcony bars to the old green men beyond
(I try to re-establish some previous connection)
I must break free of all bonds
(constructed on blind rainy afternoons in the
coffee-muddled brain)
seeing brick and mortar, not as prisons,
but mind sets, not fire escapes,
but stairways to heaven for cats
and other roof-dwelling mammals
not to envy the gulls, but to emulate them
not to walk among the trees
but to feel the sap pulsing through my own branches
letting my hair fall out in October with no regrets,

to breathe deep as a gust of wind
or sculpt the body of my thoughts
like some recalcitrant Rodin
in an imaginary boathouse
conjuring a reunion with love

what is this fear of the business suit
that buckles me onto my knees?
Does flannel not come from sheep?

Someday, floating in a long white skirt
alone –

down some stone path.
strong, soft, successful,
peaceful and matronly
but still the glint of erotic dreams in my green eyes,
(a yellow sleep mote in one corner the tape recorder of
my dreams)

forging a letter in my mind
to some distant colleague…

After my stroll, coffee at the window, over my desk,
self-sufficient, thought – full, garden-drunk, tame
(in a way)
Full, to bursting with book-thoughts and leaf-art,
Full, to overflowing with passion and poetry,
Full,
Full,
Full.

August 1983

Symphony of Nothing about Sartre

Sartre drove his cart
over the bones
of being

God, before he died, came up with
nothing
the concept

things were overrated
anyway

but can we really think of no thing
just empty
ness?

(the existential chicks have flown the *coup de gras*)

Sartre drove his cart to Simone's house
in the late blind afternoon
was that nothing?

no(thing)
existed

who can really think of nothing?

Zen mastercraftsmen and
dead beetlenuts
sing its praises
in their nothing robes
kneeling in no prayer
no thought
just funny sandals
and orange cummerbunds

is that nothing?

To live and die in a thing –
that is the question

have you ever been in a thing?
or been a thing?
to someone, perhaps,
somewhere, how, why and what

maybe things have thoughts – like
but they're just much slower than ours – like
SOMEthing
ANYthing
THING-ma-jig
that's a 'thing' dance

how can you deny "that" to a that?

'thing' to me only
with thine I and I will 'not' with mine

so, in conclusion,
within things,
around things
among things

nothingness
is
dead
sorry, Sartre

ding, dong
nothing is dead

the wicked empty nothing witch
has fallen from the tower
of 'cogito ergo sum'
and is melting
melting, melting
into nothing's nothing nest

I don't believe in nothing
any more

crescendo!

July 1998

Wounded

How parched the wounded skin of the red
Tasmanian earth;
gum tree branches,
once splayed like Queen Anne's Lace
now drying into grey statues
from loneliness
on wheat-coloured sun-dried hills

the only sign of wombats, wallabies, echidnas,
devils, roos,
lumps of bloodied fur
on the dead roadside

Magpies argue the passing of so much strange
dangerous life
while Kookaburras laugh ironically – ha ha ha ka ka –

Koalas sleep like peaceful Buddhas
perched on dry snags in the park;
the Currawong sings his melodic jingle-ad tune
from rooftop antennas
in cheerful denial of the relentless drought,

and pale yellow Easter lilies grow wild
like celebratory trumpets of life
in the dark dry eucalypt woods

as if
the clouds that pass over
without ever dropping rain
and the sun that burns so hot it bores a hole
in the Earth's halo
and makes human skin erupt like porridge,
were merely passing trends –

but the dry land still quietly screams
as if
the Earth itself felt remorse for the time when the
original people were called a blight on the landscape
and had to be removed.

While the wounded land cries out for someone to notice
it's dying of thirst,

the magpies' haunting warble
whistles through my ears

as the earth awakes

whoodle do whee do whup.

March 2000 / Hobart, Tasmania

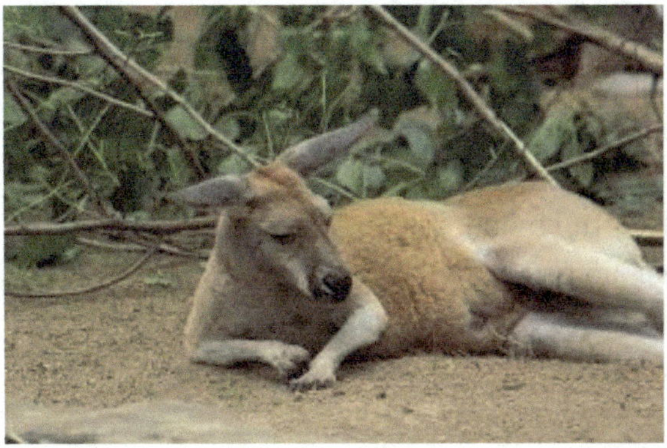

The Foggy Ant People who Forgot

After The Great Judgment, the fog cleared…

Under a full moon, The Trickster hops around the last human body,
sniffing like Coyote, lifting his leg, saying
"Now, what have we here?"
He looks up
noticing the fiery reaches of distant stars
feeling the winds of unstable suns
blowing through his spirit
which was never disturbed – and always there.

Normally given to laughter but capable of great seriousness,
face impassive, features still,
he contemplates the meaning of it…

"What happened?" he wonders.

A voice in the wind replies,
"They never listened to the grandmothers inside"

forgot they were ants –
got caught up in the notion of 'individualism'
forgot they were tribal people living in an atribal world.

imperial scientists, invaders,
kept breaking things down,
dissecting, labeling,
forgot the 'whole'.
(an ant never thinks only of itself
and how it can get ahead of the others
it works for the colony)

But they placed themselves above all creatures
(failed to recognize the ant within),
above the Earth they forgot was home –
devoured all, like termites,
without compassion

forgot they were an orchestra
not meant to play solo
but sang the song of usury and profit
danced for Darwin and Freud

forgot to ask the 'People-Whose-Moccasins-have-Puckered-Seams'
how to pray – in the old way.

Aggression (from fear
from loss of spirit)
became their anthem
as they marched alone

toward their doom.

Raven stood under the Tree of Peace in moonlight,
thinking,
"They could have lived one hundred thousand years
helped the Earth to become herself
to bloom under the fiery stars,
her kin,

transform her into
a shining star."

November, 1999

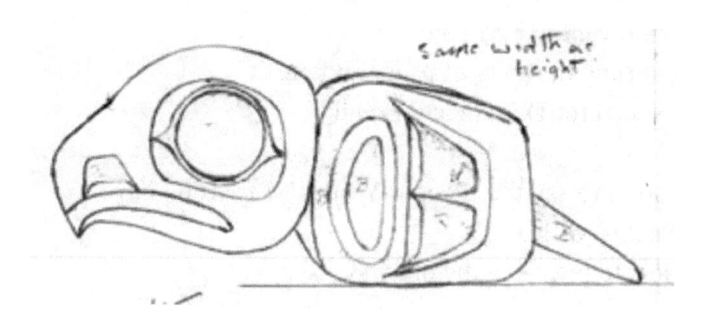

Gorby's Revolution

Gorby's revolution goes around and around and around. The dialectic is dyslexic, is merely a change of hats – and all the puppets dance. We on the left are what's left, by the road, the shop, the tree. We thought the experiment was noble until it began to spin. From the penthouse to the street, not much but rain trickles down. It's the order of things, they say: everyone wants to better himself

Gorby's resolution, Gorby's devolution goes round and round and round. There is a man on the street huddled in a storefront alcove; tall, dark, and overcoated, he looks like the reincarnation of Rabindranath Tagore. More and more they ask me for my final fifty cents. I hustle by as quickly as a car, pretending not to notice. You've got to be careful, people say, there are so many thieves about. I guess they need it more than I do. I guess they think I don't care.

All the superpowers have their good old boys and all the number-crunchers skim a little here and there and everyone's trying to better herself as the world spins sadly to a hard core. Gorby tried to rid the world of weapons (Gorby saw the victims of Chernobyl) but Reagan refused to give up his Star Toys and the mad puppets all asked "How high?"

The little cat nestling close has no idea what I'm scratching here, she just purrs and purrs while somewhere a government is being toppled, a leader assassinated, and a rich man robbed. And an old man in a tattered coat tries to sleep in a winter alcove (his white breath steaming from his mouth like a cloud of guilt) adjusting his head on the stone step for comfort, visions of grimacing marionettes gavotting in his head.

January 19, 2000

Hey Nonny Arabesque

And as for the purple travesty of light, let it fall on all
Adams, thighs, maidens, warlocks and wild garlands. I
give up, give into, give over – all dark possession into
youthful beauty and lissome lithe...
bonny and blithe (and good and gay) the spirit runs
afraid of too much happiness on such sweet south
street short notice – o go wan.

Now it comes at last, from the mysterious place, the
dirigible deluge of drowsy drops, all
on
a
raucous rooftop
rat-a-tat-tat,
pitty pat, pitty pat –

like a thousand fingers tapping softly on the skin, little
hammers, little triggers, little sniggers, distant love...
or dancing figures

waiting... waiting – the dark net in my black tower
stockings, stalking the elusive image like a stone...
a hammersmith
here's your clash cliché, your lion lily, your avant
barge big stuff, *popularos* party favour, don't do me
any – please – I don't aim to – hi, never swallowed any

thready trends 'til now... I've sold out the sideshow, brought the house down

lit the heights of artifice, arty faces – yikes! Hey nonny nonny. More moonlight. Go figure.

July 22, 2000

O Please Don't

O please don't let me read another poem about lovers,
of the cradling of heads and limbs in arms,
the restful sleep that comes to lovers
is distant as a summer storm

the squall has gone –

in that weather map of memories I recall
the flower-tipped ecstasies of love
like the arms of sea anemones
squirming blissfully at the sea's touch…

envelopment

the joyful journey from lusty fury to spent dream

the savouring of a favourite wisp of hair
a lingering look (the drowning liquid mystery in eyes)

the mutual reading of a book in bed,
our skyship, launched to infinity among the clouds,

exchange of verse we offered up like gifts
savouring the sound of him forming your words
in his mouth
like ripe cherries of meaning and intent,

– loving our creations as if they were our children –

And as we finally gently lay asleep askew,
the spirit world slept right beside us,
on the very edges of our happy hides
whispering its comforts into our drowsy ears

(now in the dark shallows of a solitary pool
the woman becomes the little girl,
lost like Scarlet in the fog,
fighting sharks of guilt in mixed-up dreams,
astonished at the repetition of alone)

so, please don't show me another poem about lovers
cradling each other in their limpet arms
I was a dancing pink sea anemone
who loved the storm

November 27, 1999

The Great Wall: Fin de Siècle

Coming up to the third millennium –
two thousand years –
three hundred and sixty-five (times) two thousand
(equals)
seven hundred and thirty thousand days –
each day a life
each life a song
each song a poem
each poem a story

hard to believe I've been here
that long
feel like
some obscure character in a history book
or… a point of paint in a picture by Seurat
feels like
approaching a big dark wall
with a tiny door in it
through which, if you know the secret code
or whose name to say sent you,
you may enter.

The wall has a big bright light behind it
and a busy schedule of agendas to sort through

but if you stay focused

and try not to see / be/ everything
in all its pro (fusion),
con (fusion),
ill (usion) –
swimming in Lilburn's 'ungraspable diversity of here;
flicking by so fast
so furrily fast, yet so pointilistically,
like blips on a computer screen, or music video edits,
you may continue the journey

double-clicking through time,
watching the high-speed chaos parade
for a little while longer

adding more zeroes to your name,

still seeking that illusive storm-eye of still.

Nov. 27, 1999

A Faint Roar

Behind the din of modern clink and clang.
the old man hears a faint roar building,
behind the strains of Challiapin's *Onegin,*
it fills him – the applause!

Once for him –
now for his ancient Russian idol –
(haunted by ghosts of vocal greatness
no one else has ever heard).

Beneath the too-large table
in the tiny social-housing flat,
his two tired feet warm and rest
in one large sheepskin slipper,
scratching tirelessly the pile of lotto tickets
he studies beneath the dimming lamp,
poring over and over the numbers,
breaking them down like a scientist,
analyzing them like an opera score,
scratching, scratching, scratching,
like a deafened dog whose fleas
dried up a long time ago,
their invisible carcasses mingling with carpet dust –
a miniature Flanders Field
around the slipper fortress.

The growing silence has become shrill
for the ninety-four-year-old Dublin baritone
whose *Iago* once raged across the stages of Europe
though now he can't hear his daughter screaming
not to forget his gloves as he leaves too early for church –
the place he trudges to every day, on withering legs,
hedging his bets against The Grim One,

his main opponent in this Game of Chance.

Behind the screen of modern images,
TV, pop music, videos,
there is another world
he can see when his tired mind
begins to drift from important ticket-work
and his head falls, his eyes close:
there it is!
the orchestra tuning up at rehearsal,
beautiful women in jewels and fur-trimmed gowns,
singers, extras, taking their places on the stage,
the sparkle and gleam of gaslight chandeliers,
burgundy-velvet-cushioned chairs along the mezzanine,
the maestro lifting his baton.
Soon all the elements come together
and he is downstage centre,
singing from the bottom of his being,

like a child – who 'never makes a mistake with the voice'
placing himself in the hands of God,
letting the great music flow through him.

Behind the clink and clang of modern city life,
there is the blessed silence, the refuge,
for it is only in this sanctuary that
the old baritone can hear the faint roar building.

January 12, 2000.

The Hall of the Drunken Fairies

That night, we went over to the Hall of the Drunken Fairies to celebrate our victory; the fireflies were dancing around our heads, lighter than air, like a thousand little moon-blossoms, mite-sized consciousnesses of light – a strange substance that can and cannot be held… It was a magic night – with all the doorways and windows emitting an orange-amber glow made by the gaslight and candle lanterns inside every home and shop.

Many fascinating characters danced and dangled there: ghost dancers, masked-men, poets, musicians, thespians, Burmese marionettes with gold and silver faces, even the living Bodhisattva herself. We drank rice and cherry wine from blue and white china teacups, told stories, laughed and sang into the deep of night (evening stretched into night like a cat goddess splaying her mink-grey torso into pure comfort, languishing on jade velvet pillows surrounded by little fat-bellied figures carved in ivory, ebony, and gold – soft and mysterious in the lanterns' glow).

Home. Our little houseboat had a curved wooden roof and two kerosene lamps hanging from the makeshift ceiling and the monkeys leapt with joy and curiosity upon our return; one leapt so far, he fell splashing into the rocking water, which later licked and lapped gently against the sides of the wooden hull like a giant liquid jellyfish.

We huddled close together in our small hard bed, happy to have found each other at last, dreaming of the beauty in the world, rocking like two sleepy drunken fairies. No more wishes necessary.

Stardust Memories

Everybody wants to be a star
to glint and sparkle with the TV set,
to gleam and glow like light under lights
to show they're worth paying attention to

But is that such a nasty thing?
(the odor of ambition often a distasteful smell)
maybe Arthur C. Clarke was right
when he agreed with RM Rilke and Mr. Hesse

Maybe deep down everybody knows
we come from stars
and our true vocation
is transformation

to burn so bright we help the Earth achieve
her ultimate goal of invisibility
to shine so strong,
we burn ourselves out, too.

July 2, 2000

Oh Cat

Oh cat
your glistening gelatinous green eyes
have diamond black pupils
with one white star in each
where the light catches the liquid surface
but who stares so intently through those black-holes?
what unfathomable mind beholds me
with such intense fascination?

Behind those black pools lies the mystery of the universe

What consciousness holds me fixed in its gaze?
is so spellbound by mine?

All animals have mind, are clever – more than human –
psychic, know what you're thinking
before you do

and they love us – not only because we feed them
they seem to have no choice
it's natural for them to love us

must we all love that which is more powerful than us
because we depend on it?

but – while that may be true for a domestic cat
it doesn't hold with an elephant, or a great ape.

Animals sense those who don't love them
and either avoid them, attack them, or try to win them
over – with the kind of silent patient empathy and
devotion only animals seem capable of.

Cats are always wild – so when they love you,
it's an honour.

Less blindly devoted than dogs,
they can keep their distance
even when they have no one but you,

know the secret of independence
better than any human.

If each species has its own evolution,
cats are advanced –
living vehicles of the universal love
and wisdom that's in us all
but which humans so often forget, abandon, betray.

July 99

Argillite I

one day beaver
erupted from stone
teeth flat promising
hands on both sides
fingers pointing down
froze there in proper position
staring
for all eternity
out
at skillful hands that
carved him
smirked at his mortal creator
thinking of his own immortality

above
large beak protruded
from human-eyed face
(but eyes are eyes)
argillite is earth

with abalone casings
fitted over eyes
his vision became translucent
and multi-coloured

above

wings swept out on both sides
like flags
perfect in asymmetry
strength of statement
purpose, heraldic

witness to human sunset
out there…

dance of life that moves
tragicomic
across real horizon
he once knew

at once the eagle
next

Nov. 2000

Faunic Triptych

I – shuffling buffalo

this aging Cherokee man... on TV
talking about the early movement west of the Cherokee
relocation really:
forced relocation = movement,
i.e., not of their own Buffalo free Bill...
this getting old Cherokee man
was talking, I say,
about what the buffalo meant to his people

sacred, he said,
like *gods* to the elders...
yes, we killed them, used their whole bodies for our
sustenance:
hides for tepees, blankets, moccasins; meat for food;
bones: tools, jewellery, drumsticks... peace
and other parts for medicine
only Medicine Men knew about
buffalo were the scaffolding of our lives...

so, yes, we killed our own gods
but so did you, remember?
(your own long-haired one who tried to teach love)

But the white man was ordered to shoot hundreds,
thousands of our gods
[Buffalo Bill once bragged he killed 4,280 head
in seventeen months]
[brag] [adagio] all but five hundred –
and those were up in Canada –

after the slaughter, the Cherokee man said,
the old people were lost, their spirits, their minds.
Crazy.
Never recovered.

II freedom

The Ainu of Japan had certain beliefs regarding bears:
(whom they killed to survive)
believing this world more attractive than the next,
the Ainu thought bears were spirit beings from another
world trapped in bear bodies,
orphaned here on Earth for a time, their animal
appearance a uniform they had to don in order to come
here. Once they put them on, they couldn't remove
them of their own accord. They needed humans to help
set them free so they could return home.

So the story goes...

They'd kidnap a bear cub, take him into their village,
raise him as their own [allow him to play with the
children until he reached the age when he got too
rough]. Then the head of the household would prepare
the cub for the occasion, saying:

*Little divinity... we are about to send you home and in
case you have never experienced one of these
ceremonies before, you must know that it has to be
this way. We want you to go home and tell your
parents how well you have been treated here on Earth.
And if you have enjoyed your life among us and would
like to do us the honour of coming to visit again, we in
turn shall do you the honour of arranging for another
ceremony of this kind.* *

elaborate ritual celebration for the slaughter
the people dance and sing with happiness for their little
charge
because they're about to set him free,
return him to his original home and family in the next
world.

III the power of speech

'orangutan' the word stands colossal, a monument,
even when referentless (but no less reverent):

Orang = man, utan = forest

Orang = orange – the colour of these fantastic brethren
with inveigling smiles fading…
the natives of Borneo believe 'the man from the forest'
could talk to us if he wanted to – but, fascinatingly,
prefers not to.

Perhaps these thoughtful creatures with wise childlike
faces are afraid of what they might say to their human
cousins. Hardly blame them.

Orange Malaysian Cousin, wistful in repose,
I re-*cognize* you
can I come and swing with you in your green world?

High above the traveling Buffalo Bill show?

* Joseph Campbell, Myths to Live By - *Jan. 27, 20*

London: Impressions

Now, London is what I call a city! London is: the feeling on Fleet Street: long navy wool coats and fluttering red scarves waiting for double tall red buses in the bitter wind, figures moving like quick brush strokes in a grey sped-up film, huddling in bus shelters to keep warm; the sudden Dickens of the side-lanes and old narrow houses all connected in rows but with different architectural features – overhanging, Tudor-beamed top rooms, glowering gargoyles on doorframes, archways leading to other narrow lanes and secret worlds with hanging pub signs clattering in the gusts.

We found the entrance to Ye Olde Cheshire Cheese on one such narrow lane, the famous pub in which Samuel Johnson once ate his lunch and sipped his pints, quill pen scratching paper in the tiny darkened rooms up the narrow winding stairs, old paintings and oak wainscoting blackened by centuries of cigar smoke and coal soot. The effect was of gas lighting. No women in the front room – only men… just as it had been in Johnson's day

The weathered vendors near Petticoat Lane, closing up shop, proud to give us directions to the famous street among the every-which-way labyrinth they knew as home. Back in the Fleet Street lawyers' pub, The George, black and white faces in more long navy coats (black shoes) – the legal profession rushing into the bar for their after-work pint, talking on cell phones, chatting with colleagues about affairs of the day, across from the Royal Courts of Justice. Kentucky Fried Chicken on the railway station steps, one bas-relief gargoyle face above the door grinning menacingly down on us.

The pub names alone are worth the price of admission, like little poems or book titles: Dirty Dick's, The Tipperary, The Slurping Toad, The Wig & Pen, Ye Olde Cocke Inn (fittingly a gay bar), The Prospect of Whitby (near Wapping), The Prince of Wales' Feathers,

The Bull & Staff, The Wat Tyler, The Malt Shovel, The Red Lion, The Sherlock Holmes, The Admiral Hardy, The Paper Moon. Pretty pub-maids, little English boys and girls with moppet hair, wide eyes and articulate speech who talk like miniature grown-ups in perfect clipped English phrases, some with accents from the north or south. The names of train-stops, little histories: Eltham, Sidcup, Bexleyheath, Bethnal Green, Hampton Wick, Greenwich, Falconwood, Waterloo, and Charing Cross – the hub, where all tracks meet and fly off again, north and south, east and west.

On the boat tour up the Thames, the comedian commentator regales us with gruesome tales of the skirmishes, wars and beheadings that made London what she is today. He giggles to himself as he relates the story of how John Cuckold had a special wire cage built for his unfaithful wife in which to lower her into the bitterly cold Thames, as punishment for her infidelity. This practice became all the rage in its day, he says, gloatingly. The old *Queen Mary*, once the grandest of all sailing ships, now sits idle and seems small after the whole world has seen the *Titanic* on the big screen. The Prospect of Whitby, quaint old pub hanging above the river, has a four-hundred-year-old bar and brilliant 'bangers and mash'. And now the famous London Bridge and 'Bloody Tower' loom in the distance, as we sail into the centre of the great city. St. Paul's high-vaulted gold-leaf ceiling splendour with its Byzantine designs, made up of a hundred four-way arches and statues of dead bishops and war honourees. Five hundred and sixty steps to get up to the walkway around the ceiling. One soon begins to see also that it is the unique vision of the great Christopher Wren that gives London her grandiose splendour.

London is prose, scattered with isolated spots of poetry – all detail, deliberation, décor, decorum, grandeur and pomp; buildings built for kings and queens, square and curved linear spaces meant for sovereigns, with the dirty poor scattered on the streets like bits of crumpled paper blown about by the blustering winds that roar through open converging squares: Leicester, Trafalgar, Piccadilly, Warren Street, Covent Garden. Cornices, gables, monoliths, steps, pillars, flying buttresses and Gothic spires; Ionic columns, fluted stonework, leaded windows, some tiny, some huge, (the tiny-windowed towers) insignia, gargoyles, coats of arms, statues of men on horseback. From the train, one can see the chimney-top world where cats and thieves once roamed, huge spires and rotundas looming up behind iron-gated structures. Gazing at all this, one is hit by the realization that it was in these buildings that monumental legal and financial decisions were made that once affected the entire world; a sense of the power this city once wielded infuses everything. Especially, the great cathedrals, the Houses of Parliament, curved streets and detailed buildings, the posh old hotels – the Savoy, the Waldorf, looking so huge and grand with their red-and-black-clad doormen and big dark-green awnings to shut out the riffraff. Soho, whose narrow winding alleys were once the home of artists and writers, now seems reduced to a circus of sex shops and porn video houses. As we board the train to Oxford – to tread where Shakespeare trod – I look back at that great homage to the imagination, London Town, and think: finally, I have seen a real CITY!

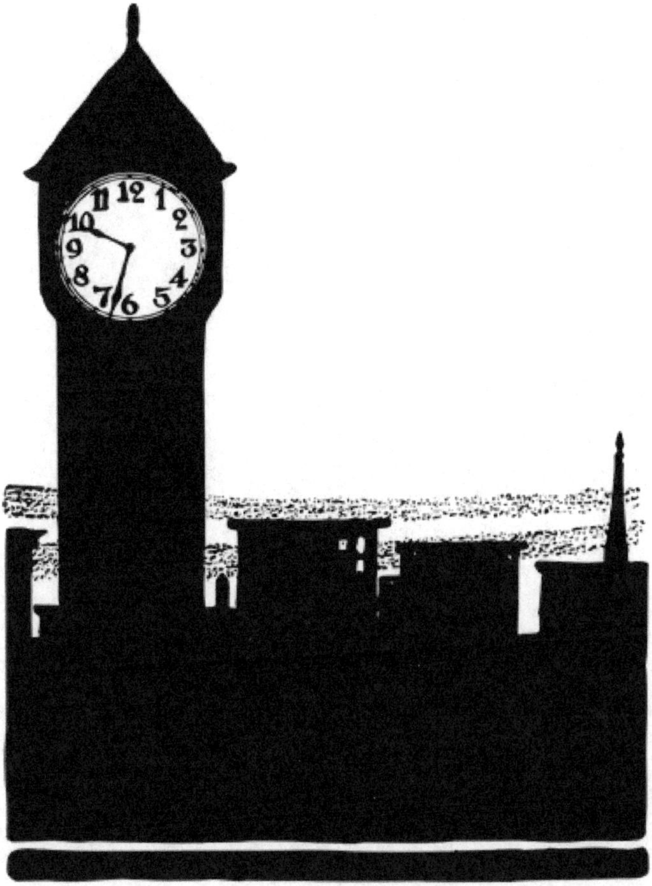
12
1
2
3
4
5
6
7
8
9
10
11